REMARKABLE

CANADIANS

Sir John A.
Macdonald

by Rebecca Szulhan

Published by Weigl Educational Publishers Limited
6325 – 10 Street SE
Calgary, Alberta, Canada
T2H 2Z9

Website: www.weigl.com

Library and Archives Canada Cataloguing in Publication

Szulhan, Rebecca
    Sir John A. Macdonald / Rebecca Szulhan.

(Remarkable Canadians)
Includes index.
ISBN 978-1-55388-319-7 (bound)
ISBN 978-1-55388-320-3 (pbk.)

    1. Macdonald, John A. (John Alexander), 1815-1891--Juvenile literature.
2. Prime ministers--Canada--Biography--Juvenile literature. 3. Canada--Politics
and government--1867-1896--Juvenile literature. I. Title. II. Series.

FC521.M3S98 2007   j971.05'1092   C2006-906256-0

Printed in the United States of America
1 2 3 4 5 6 7 8 9 0 11 10 09 08 07

Editor: Liz Brown
Design: Terry Paulhus

We acknowledge the financial support of the Government of Canada through the Book
Publishing Industry Development Program (BPIDP) for our publishing activities.

Cover: John A. Macdonald was Canada's first prime minister.

Photograph Credits
Cover: Archives Canada (C-008963); Archives Canada: pages 8 (PA-062177), 10
(c000733), 13 bottom right (c-001971), 19 (PA-144822), 20 (C-021597); Glenbow
Archives: pages 5 (na-293-2), 16 (na-293-3); Registered by the Government of Ontario
under the Trade Marks Act: page 7 top left; Ontario Archives: pages 14 (I0001199),
15 (I0001528).

Every reasonable effort has been made to trace ownership and to obtain permission
to reprint copyright material. The publishers would be pleased to have any errors
or omissions brought to their attention so that they may be corrected in
subsequent printings.

Contents

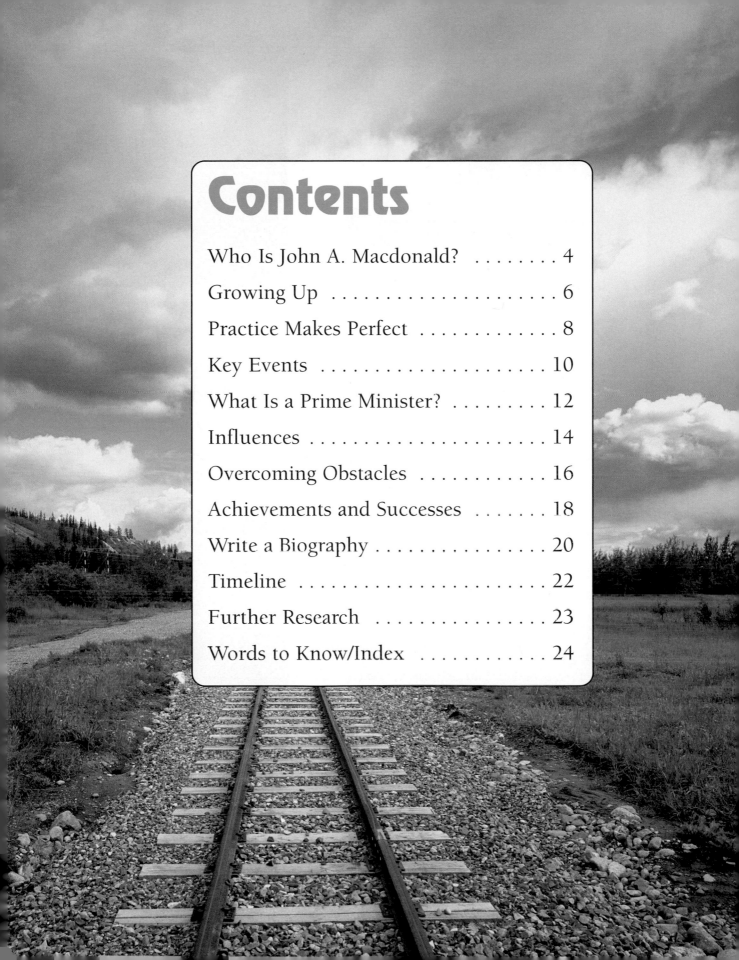

Who Is John A. Macdonald?

Sir John Alexander Macdonald was Canada's first **prime minister**. He was a **lawyer** and a **politician**. John is also known as one of the Fathers of **Confederation**. The Fathers of Confederation were a group of politicians who helped bring the provinces of Canada together as one country.

"I have tried, according to the best of my judgment, to do what I could for the well-being of good government and the future prosperity of this, my beloved country."

John wanted to bring the people of Canada closer together. To do this, he oversaw the building of a railroad that stretched across Canada. This railroad made it easier for Canadians to trade goods and travel throughout the country. As prime minister, John worked hard to make Canada a country where many different people could be happy.

Growing Up

John Alexander Macdonald was born on January 10, 1815, in Glasgow, Scotland. His parents were Hugh and Helen Macdonald. Hugh was a businessman. Helen loved to read and taught her children that education was important. John had one brother, James, and two sisters, Margaret and Louisa. When John was five years old, his family moved from Scotland to Canada.

John's family settled in Kingston, Ontario. His uncle, Donald Macpherson, lived there. In Kingston, John attended the Midland District Grammar School. Later, he attended the John Cruickshank School. At school, reading was one of John's favourite activities. When he was 15 years old, John left school and began training to become a lawyer at a local law firm.

🍁 Glasgow is the largest city in Scotland. More than 500,000 people live in Glasgow.

Ontario Tidbits

COAT OF ARMS

MINERAL
Amethyst

FLOWER
White Trillium

Toronto is the provincial capital.

The largest freshwater island in the world is in Ontario. It is called Manitoulin Island, and it is located in Lake Huron.

Kingston, Ontario, was the capital of Canada until 1844.

There are more than 12 million people living in Ontario.

Ottawa, Ontario, is the capital of Canada.

Think about it!

Sir John A. Macdonald grew up in Kingston, Ontario. Research Kingston's history. How do you think growing up in Kingston influenced Sir John's decision to work in politics?

Practice Makes Perfect

John **articled** in the Kingston law office of George Mackenzie. During the day, John would write letters and do legal research for George. At night, he would study to learn all that he could about law. George was impressed with John's work. When George died in 1835, John opened his own law office. In Kingston, John was known as a good lawyer. His office handled many cases. John was interested in a career in politics because he wanted to make important decisions about his town and country.

In the 1800s, Kingston was the largest town in Upper Canada.

In 1844, John was elected to be a member of the **legislative assembly** of the Province of Canada. The Province of Canada had been created by Great Britain in 1841. It united Upper Canada with Lower Canada. In 1867, Ontario and Quebec became separate provinces.

In the legislative assembly, John represented the town of Kingston and the **Conservative** party. By 1854, he had become **attorney general**. In 1857, John became **co-premier** of the Province of Canada with George-Étienne Cartier.

John and George-Étienne found it difficult to govern the Province of Canada. Cultural and religious differences between the English- and French-speaking people made it difficult to make laws in the government. Between 1861 and 1864, there were two elections and three different governments in the province.

It was a political **deadlock**. John and George-Étienne believed that Confederation would help solve many of the problems that the Province of Canada faced.

George-Étienne Cartier worked in politics with John for almost 20 years. He is considered one of the Fathers of Confederation.

Key Events

In 1864, John, George-Étienne, and a politician named George Brown began to work together to bring about Confederation. This was called the Great Coalition of 1864. The coalition wanted the Province of Canada to separate into two different provinces called Ontario and Quebec. Each province would have its own government for local matters. There would be a central government in Ottawa that would make **national** decisions. In 1867, Ontario and Quebec became separate provinces.

The coalition wanted the four colonies on the Atlantic coast of Canada to join Confederation. On September 1, 1864, they travelled to the city of Charlottetown, Prince Edward Island, to meet with politicians from these colonies. John made many speeches. He tried to convince the other colonies to join Confederation. The politicians agreed to meet with the coalition again in Quebec City in October. After the October meeting, New Brunswick and Nova Scotia agreed to join Confederation. On July 1, 1867, Canada became the first **dominion** in the British Empire. A month later, John was chosen as Canada's first prime minister.

🍁 The Charlottetown meetings were held between September 1 and 9, 1864. Many of the men who gathered at the meetings became friends.

Thoughts from John

John worked hard to create the nation of Canada. Here are some of the things he said about the country and people.

John talks about his hopes for the railway.

"It will give us a great, a united, a rich, an improving, a developing Canada."

John tells a crowd about the benefits of his policies.

"You are all richer, you have better looking hats, and better looking coats."

John describes the people of Canada.

"I can trust...the **patriotism** of this country."

John is proud to be prime minister.

"I feel great pride in occupying the position that has been awarded me by the people of this country."

At the end of his career, John reflects about his work.

"I have had a long life of politics, and a long life of...duties."

John talks about working as a politician.

"I have said again and again that the two most uncertain things in the world are an election and a horse race."

What Is a Prime Minister?

A prime minister is the political leader of Canada. Each of Canada's **political parties** has a leader. These leaders **campaign** for the position of prime minister. Then, Canadians vote for the party they feel will best meet their needs. The leader of the party that receives the most votes becomes prime minister.

A prime minister has many duties. One of the prime minister's duties is to meet with the premiers. The prime minister and premiers meet to discuss the needs of the provinces. The prime minister must meet with leaders from other countries to discuss global issues. Prime ministers are involved in decision making that affects all Canadians.

Stephen Harper became Canada's 22nd prime minister on February 6, 2006.

Prime Ministers 101

Pierre Trudeau (1919–2000)
Years in Office 1968–1979 and 1980–1984
Political Party Liberal
Achievements Pierre Trudeau created a new, Canadian-controlled Constitution. Before Trudeau, Canada's Constitution was controlled by Great Britain. Trudeau also promoted bilingualism, or the use of two languages, in Canada. He did this through the Official Languages Act. This act made French and English the two official languages of Canada.

Kim Campbell (1947–)
Years in Office 1993
Political Party Progressive Conservative
Achievements Kim Campbell began her term when Prime Minister Brian Mulroney retired from office. She was the first female Canadian prime minister. During her political career, Campbell made amendments to the criminal code in areas such as firearms control.

Lester Pearson (1897–1972)
Years in Office 1963–1968
Political Party Liberal
Achievements In 1957, Lester Pearson was awarded a Nobel Peace Prize. This was in recognition of his idea to create an international peacekeeping force for the United Nations. While in office, Pearson created the Canadian **Pension Plan**. He oversaw the creation of the modern Canadian flag while he was prime minister.

Sir Wilfrid Laurier (1841–1919)
Years in Office 1896–1911
Political Party Liberal
Achievements Sir Wilfrid Laurier was Canada's first **Francophone** prime minister. Laurier promoted the interests of both French and English-speaking Canadians. During Laurier's time as prime minister, he oversaw the building of more railways in the West. These railways allowed many people to move to western Canada.

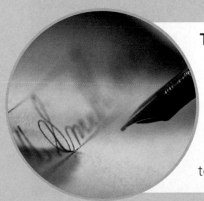

The Constitution
The Constitution is a very important document to Canadians. It is a list of guidelines that prime ministers use to make decisions that are fair. The Constitution contains the laws and rules that prime ministers must know to run the country. John was one of the authors of the Constitution. The Constitution was controlled by Great Britain until Canada took control of it through the Constitution Act of 1982.

Influences

Many people and events influenced John throughout his life. John's mother, Helen, loved to learn. She especially enjoyed reading. Helen shared these skills with John and his siblings. Throughout his life, John enjoyed reading. John's parents encouraged him to set goals and work hard to achieve them. His father told people that one day John would be "the star" of Canada.

When John was 14 years old, he joined the Law Society of Upper Canada. He wanted to train to be a lawyer. At George Mackenzie's law office, John learned a great deal. George was John's **mentor**. He taught him about law and responsibility. George even let John live in his home.

🍁 Many lawyers in Kingston, including John, worked at the Frontenac County courthouse.

John learned many lessons from George and his wife, Sarah. One of the lessons he learned was that it is important to be on time for work. John liked to sleep late in the mornings. He was sometimes late for work. One day, Sarah decided not to wake John. When he woke up, he realized that it was the end of the day, and he had missed an entire day's work. After that, John made sure that he was on time for work every day.

George influenced John's political beliefs. While John worked in his office, George told him about his ideas. George believed that the government should help businesses. When John entered politics, he held this same view.

GEORGE MACKENZIE

George Mackenzie, his wife Sarah, and their son lived in Kingston, Ontario. George was a successful lawyer. He hoped to campaign for a job as a politician in the provincial legislature. Although he was nominated, George was not able to campaign in the election. He became sick with cholera, an infection in the stomach. George died of the disease in 1835.

John and George practised law in a simple office. There were no computers, so they had to write many documents by hand.

Overcoming Obstacles

John overcame many obstacles in his lifetime. He experienced hardships in his personal life and in his political career. Despite these hardships, John experienced many successes.

In 1843, John married Isabella Clark. They had two sons named John, Jr., and Hugh John. John, Jr. died when he was 13 months old. In 1857, Isabella became sick and died. These two deaths greatly saddened John. For the rest of his life, he kept a box of John, Jr.'s toys.

John had to overcome obstacles in his political career. As prime minister, John oversaw the building of the Canadian Pacific Railway. In 1873, he accepted money from businessmen. In return, he promised that they could build the railroad. When people learned about these deals, they became upset. John was forced to resign as prime minister in 1873. These events were known as the Pacific Scandal.

🍁 John's second wife was named Susan Agnes Bernard. They married in 1867.

John did not let this ruin his career. In 1878, he campaigned for the position of prime minister again. He promised voters that he had a plan to help Canadian businesses. This was called the National Policy. John's campaign was successful. Voters elected John as prime minister once again. John remained prime minister until his death in 1891.

🍁 John had to travel to many places, such as Toronto, to give speeches during his campaign.

Achievements and Successes

John experienced much success during his career as a lawyer and politician. In 1867, Queen Victoria of Great Britain **knighted** John in recognition of his work in support of Confederation. This is why he has the title "Sir."

As a politician, John had dreamed of a country that would stretch from coast-to-coast. In 1867, John gave orders to begin building the Intercolonial Railway. The railway was finished in 1876. It ran from Truro, Nova Scotia, to Ste. Flavie, Quebec.

🍁 The Dominion of Canada was created during Queen Victoria's time. She was queen of Great Britain from 1837 to 1901.

By 1871, Manitoba and British Columbia had joined Confederation. John decided to extend the railway to connect these provinces with the rest of Canada. Construction of the Canadian Pacific Railway (CPR) began in 1875 and was finished in 1885. The CPR began at Fort William, Ontario, and ended at Craigellachie, British Columbia.

During his career, John was elected as prime minister four times. In March 1891, he was elected as prime minister for the last time. On May 29, 1891, John had a stroke. During a stroke, blood stops flowing through the brain. He became ill and had to stay in bed. On June 6, John died. He was given a state funeral. John is buried at the Cataraqui Cemetery in Kingston.

THE CANADIAN PACIFIC RAILWAY

The CPR has been transporting people and goods across Canada for more than 120 years. In 2006, the CPR collected almost $3 million and more than 700,000 kilograms of food on its Holiday Train. This train runs through the United States and Canada. It collects food and money to help people in need at Christmas. For more information about the CPR, visit www.cpr.ca.

❧ In 1886, the CPR made the first train trip from Canada's Atlantic coast to its Pacific coast.

Write a Biography

A person's life story can be the subject of a book. This kind of book is called a biography. Biographies describe the lives of remarkable people, such as those who have achieved great success or have done important things to help others. These people may be alive today, or they may have lived many years ago. Reading a biography can help you learn more about a remarkable person.

At school, you might be asked to write a biography. First, decide who you want to write about. You can choose a prime minister, such as John A. Macdonald, or any other person you find interesting. Then, find out if your library has any books about this person. Learn as much as you can about him or her. Write down the key events in this person's life. What was this person's childhood like? What has he or she accomplished? What are his or her goals? What makes this person special or unusual?

A concept web is a useful research tool. Read the questions in the following concept web. Answer the questions in your notebook. Your answers will help you write your biography.

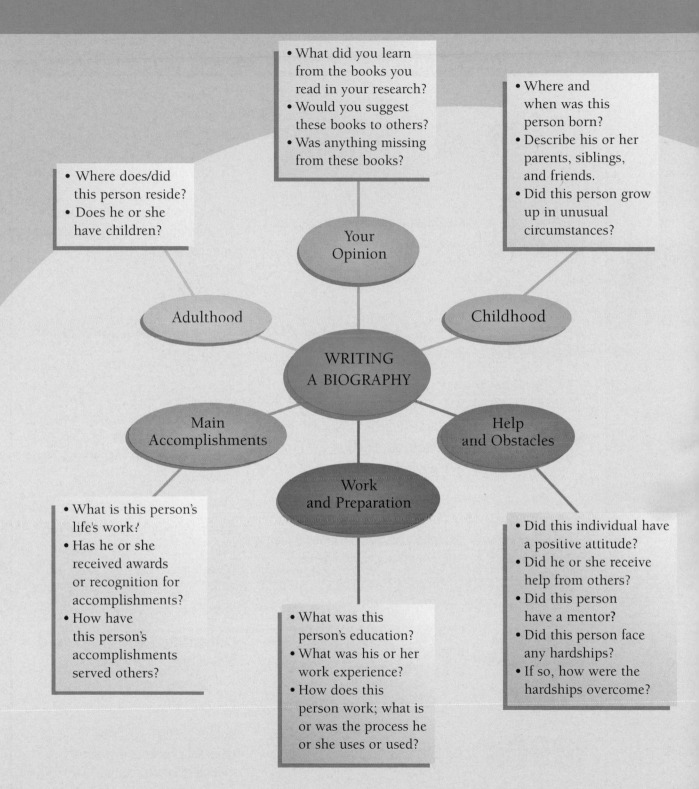

- What did you learn from the books you read in your research?
- Would you suggest these books to others?
- Was anything missing from these books?

- Where and when was this person born?
- Describe his or her parents, siblings, and friends.
- Did this person grow up in unusual circumstances?

- Where does/did this person reside?
- Does he or she have children?

Your Opinion

Adulthood

Childhood

WRITING A BIOGRAPHY

Main Accomplishments

Help and Obstacles

Work and Preparation

- What is this person's life's work?
- Has he or she received awards or recognition for accomplishments?
- How have this person's accomplishments served others?

- What was this person's education?
- What was his or her work experience?
- How does this person work; what is or was the process he or she uses or used?

- Did this individual have a positive attitude?
- Did he or she receive help from others?
- Did this person have a mentor?
- Did this person face any hardships?
- If so, how were the hardships overcome?

Timeline

DECADE	SIR JOHN A. MACDONALD	WORLD EVENTS
1810s	Sir John is born on January 10, 1815, in Glasgow, Scotland.	The United States declares war on Great Britain on June 18, 1812. The United States and France attack Britain's North American colonies. This area is now known as Canada.
1820s	The Macdonald family moves to Canada in 1820. They settle in Kingston, Ontario.	John Franklin, an explorer who mapped much of the Arctic, returns from his first trip to the Arctic in 1822.
1830s	Sir John opens his own law office in 1835.	Victoria becomes queen of Great Britain in 1837.
1840s	In 1844, Sir John is elected to the legislative assembly of the Province of Canada.	Great Britain and the United States determine the borders of Canada under the Webster-Ashburton Treaty in 1842.
1850s	Sir John's first wife, Isabella, dies in 1856 of an unknown illness.	Queen Victoria selects Ottawa to be the capital of the Province of Canada in 1857.
1860s	Sir John is elected as the first prime minister of the Dominion of Canada in 1867.	Civil War breaks out in the United States from 1861 to 1865.
1890s	Sir John dies on June 6, 1891.	Between 1891 and 1896, four different Conservative prime ministers lead Canada.

Further Research

How can I find out more about Sir John A. Macdonald?

Most libraries have computers that connect to a database for researching information. If you input a key word, you will be provided with a list of books in the library that contain information on that topic. Non-fiction books are arranged numerically, using their call number. Fiction books are organized alphabetically by the author's last name.

Websites

To learn more about Sir John A. Macdonald, visit
www.collectionscanada.ca
Type "Sir John A. Macdonald" in the search box.

To learn more about Confederation, visit
www.collectionscanada.ca/confederation/kids

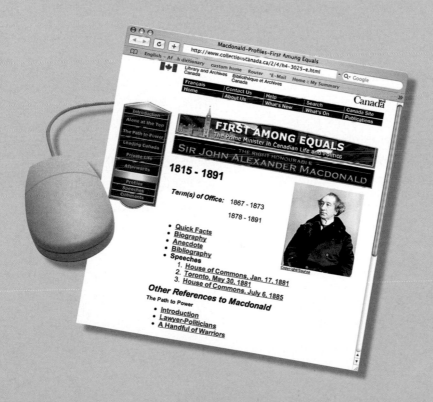

Words to Know

articled: worked to become a lawyer

attorney general: the chief law officer of Canada

campaign: gather support for an election

Confederation: when the provinces united to form Canada in 1867

Conservative: a political party in Canada

co-premier: one of two people who lead the government of a province

deadlock: impossible to act or continue because of disagreement

dominion: a self-governing country in the British Commonwealth

Francophone: someone who speaks French as his or her first language

knighted: awarded special recognition by the king or queen of Great Britain

lawyer: a person who practises law

legislative assembly: the place where provincial laws are made

mentor: a wise and trusted teacher

national: relating to the whole country

patriotism: love for one's country

pension: money given to a person who is retired, from the government

political parties: groups that have similar beliefs on how the goverment should work

politician: a person who works in politics

prime minister: the leader of Canada

Index